Prosecuting the fishery since the time of
Cabot and before, fishermen of the province
understood the meaning of the biblical
reference 'by the sweat of one's brow.'
Pre-Confederation, summer residents of
Freshwater Bay dry their catch.

PLACE OF
CHARACTER

Observing the 50th anniversary of the
entry of Newfoundland into Confederation

1949-1999

COPYRIGHT

Ennis, Ronald (John)
Falk C. (Charlie)

Cover design: Ron Ennis
Interior design: Ron Ennis

Cover photo: Durrell, Twillingate

CONTENT

DEDICATION

To the men and women who from the rich beauty and silence of their being made an incalculable contribution to our way of life...to the character of our province.

The Province of Newfoundland observes the 50th anniversary of its entry into Confederation.

On December 11, 1948 the 'Fathers of Confederation' signed the Terms of Union which would see the then-'Dominion of Newfoundland' become Canada's newest member; a feat engineered almost single-handedly by Joseph R. Smallwood.

The rightness or wrongness of the decision to join our neighbours to the west was well argued at the time, and, to a lesser degree, that decision continues to be the subject of debate today. Perhaps if there is one thing that all Newfoundlanders would agree on is that the continuity and evolution of the life of the province was changed as of March 31, 1949. As of that moment, the province's "isolation" and independence ceased to be.

And yet, as much as that might have appeared or have been measured in varying degrees as a loss or gain, the fact of the matter was, from this northerly landscape of space and time emerged a people of distinct culture and heritage. For, as the winds and seas, over a millennia of time, had chiseled shores and coastlines of distinctive ruggedness and beauty, so too had they over the centuries etched a community and people of character and determination.

In the half century that followed, it would be those people who would "open their doors" to the world; and, at times, almost naively so. But then, in all circumstances, theirs was tolerance born of a history

as a coastal people – an existence predicated by acceptance of and empathy for the 'stranger.'

From the conclaves of their often isolated existence was born a people of immense acceptance, uncanny ingenuity and titan-like resolve to exist. And, at the time of Confederation it was they – a people existing in some thirteen hundred outport communities – who would be asked to step away from their ancient way of life and into a more 'progressive' world.

TELLING THE STORY

As the Province of Newfoundland marks the anniversary year of the decision to join the confederacy of provinces called Canada, Robinson-Blackmore Printing and Publishing sees it as fitting that the story of that historic moment be told. Included in the 'chapters' that follow is a backgrounder telling something of vigorous men and women who constituted the province's population at the time; the story of the great battle and some of the main players; and then, the story about what followed – in large measure, the transformation of the people.

In presenting this written and pictorial glance of our unique history and province, there is the intent to underscore the character of our people. For, even today as we witness an exodus of families from many parts of the province to other parts of the nation, there is a strong sense that despite this new adversity

– one that has taken many to the breaking-point – this province, and its people, will survive.

And even as the fabric of our own community is being strained, we know our nation is the stronger because of the very winnowing process that is currently taking place – and has taken place over the decades. Doubtless has another race of people ever been so tested. And yet, it is from that very crucible – in large measure, moulded of geography and climate – have the qualities for survival emerged. Perhaps why on this momentous occasion can we proudly say, Newfoundland is indeed a *Place of Character*.

Ron Ennis
Managing editor,
Robinson-Blackmore Newspapers

Previous pages:
Nets piled high are fitting foreground for North America's oldest city – a city that has been, and still is today, safe haven for ships from around the world.

Clockwise, from top left:
Plumes of smoke rise from the Corner Brook mill; panoramic shot of the town of Port aux Basques, with passenger ferry in background; the lighthouse at Woody Point looks out on the Gulf of St. Lawrence; and, the Northern Peninsula town of Conche.

Pages 11-13:
Late evening - looking down from Signal Hill on the capital city of St. John's; autumn's brush turns the picturesque City of Corner Brook crimson and gold; and, the Barbour premises, Newtown.

14

Clockwise, from left:
This mid-1980s Falk photograph of Salvage is good indicator of where those who were employed in the fishery built their houses – most often on a jut of land that allowed easy access to the sea; one of the more scenic drives in the province, through the mountainous west coast region and along a section of the Trans-Canada Highway that follows, for a distance, the Humber River; and, the Labrador community of Nain.

Previous page:
The rustic setting of McIver's, Bay of Islands.

PLACE OF
CHARACTER

A product of Robinson-Blackmore Printing and Publishing,
with photography by **Charlie Falk**

Contributing writers include:

Sue Hickey
David Sorensen
Dr. Noel Murphy
Judge Robert A. Fowler

ROBINSON BLACKMORE
Printing and Publishing

CREDITS

Charlie Falk is a Gander-based photographer who, for more than two decades, has been travelling to the farthest reaches of the province recording special moments in the lives of its people.

Sue Hickey is a reporter, columnist and photographer with The Advertiser, a Robinson-Blackmore newspaper serving the Exploits Valley area of the province.

David Sorensen, a former editor (with The Beacon, Gander) and reporter with a number of Robinson-Blackmore community newspapers, is currently editor of The MUN Gazette.

Dr. Noel Murphy, president of the Humber Valley Broadcasting Company, is a freelance columnist with R-B's community newspaper in the City of Corner Brook, The Humber Log.

Judge Robert A. Fowler currently sits on the bench of the Provincial Court in the Town of Grand Falls-Windsor.

The Canada that Newfoundland chose

The title of Joey Smallwood's autobiography, *I Chose Canada*, is an implicit reminder that Canada may have opened the door to the tiny independent nation, but Newfoundland made the final decision to walk in.

Ex-Prime Minister Pierre Trudeau recognized that, stating in a collection of essays about Smallwood, *Just Call Me Joey* – "we are lucky that twenty years ago, you decided to allow Canada to join Newfoundland; we are lucky, because you almost decided not to."

Still, Newfoundlanders sometimes regard mainland Canada with distrust, and even disdain. Archaeology has proven, through the Helge and Anne Stine Ingstad's painstaking excavations at L'Anse aux Meadows on the tip of the Northern Peninsula, that Newfoundland was a highly probable candidate for the fabled Viking Vinland, and the first known site of European habitation in the New World. Columbus may have "discovered" America, but many Newfoundlanders will tell you that North American's colonization history started when John Cabot landed on Newfoundland shores in 1497 in pursuit of the legendary cod stocks possibly known to seasoned Portuguese fishermen. Couple five hundred years of history with the forging of a distinct culture over the same period of time, and you have the seeds for a healthy Newfoundland nationalism.

We were Britain's first colony in the New World, Newfoundland children are taught in school, well before the rest of Canada came into being.

Indeed, Canada's roots are in the four Atlantic provinces, from which explorers, settlers and pioneers ventured west to open up the frontiers.

SENSE OF HISTORY...

But Newfoundland's entry into Confederation in 1949 was not into a nation with no sense of history or culture.

On the contrary, Newfoundland had more in common with the Dominion than what was apparent on the surface. Newfoundland's decision to join Canada after the vote of July 22, 1948, was a close one, with 78,323 for and 71,334 against, because many in the province were wary of their loss of identity and culture as an independent nation.

It has been noted that Newfoundland is the only province of the ten to have joined Confederation by the democratically expressed will of its people

The Confederation that created Canada came about for similar reasons, as British North Americans prepared to fight for their separate political existence in North America. It was also practical: the War of 1812 had demonstrated that America had tried before to take over its northern neighbours, and the provinces were small, weak, widely separated, badly deficient in communications and vulnerable to attack.

And Newfoundland, once before, had been invited to join the new nation that was soon to be. In a letter, dated June 1867, Sir John A. Macdonald wrote to leading Newfoundland confederate, Ambrose Shea, that "by the exercise of common sense and a limited amount of that patriotism which goes by the name of self-interest, I have no doubt that Union will be good for the common weal."

Newfoundland remained apathetic, feeling that she didn't need Canada because her per capita debt at that time was only $7.28 compared to Canada's $30.13; she didn't need the railway that was so important to the mainland colonies, nor felt threatened by the militant Irish, the Fenians. Yet Canada continued to grow, and what awaited Newfoundland before Confederation was a nation now reaping the benefits of the post-war boom.

ECONOMY IMPROVES

In 1949, it was four years after the Second World War, and 20 years after the start of the Great Depression. And Canada's prosperity, two years earlier, had taken a turn for the better, with a discovery in a small Alberta village. Leduc was the place, and Alberta's fortune, based on oil and natural gas, was made. And with that discovery, all Canada seemed to start rolling.

Mines couldn't keep up with the demand from the United States. Farms couldn't keep up with the wants of a hungry, battle-scarred Europe. And forests could hardly meet the call for paper.

Titanium was produced in Quebec, potash in

Saskatchewan, and British Columbia lumber was sent to rebuild the cities, its fruit to help restore the health of other nations.

The skimping war years had brought a huge demand for consumer goods, refrigerators, cars, bathtubs for the new houses that were wanted following the baby boom of 1946 and 47.

At the head of it all was C.D. Howe, as minister of trade and commerce, urging Canada on. His energy almost dimmed an important milestone, the retirement of Mackenzie King, who had served as prime minister longer than anyone in the Commonwealth.

10TH PROVINCE

King's successor, Louis St. Laurent, soon had a feather in his cap: Newfoundland voted to become the 10th Canadian province.

But when Newfoundland joined Confederation, not every province could claim it was enjoying the era's economic prosperity. The neighbouring Maritimes scarcely prospered in the new union; even in 1949, they were only just beginning to benefit from it. Family allowances were then only five years old; unemployment insurance had been in effect only nine years. The policy of equalizing have and have-not regions across the country was still nearly a decade away.

On April 1, 1949, it was Newfoundland's turn to see what Canada had to offer. Over a CBC Radio broadcast, after the country had officially joined Confederation at 11:59 p.m. on March 31 (Joey didn't want it to be April Fools' Day), St. Laurent welcomed Newfoundland to "a good country, a country of which you will become as proud as we are...in becoming a province of Canada, you will not lose the identity of which you are so proud."

Sue Hickey

Terms of Union:
Joseph R. Smallwood signing the Terms of Union between Newfoundland and Canada, December 11, 1948 in the House of Commons Chamber in Ottawa.

• Photo courtesy of Centre for Newfoundland Studies Archives, Memorial University of Newfoundland

Adjacent page:

The arrival of the capelin in the spring of the year caused paroxysms of excitement in coastal communities. Besides being a staple for the home, it was used as bait and as a fertilizer in the kitchen garden.

Below:

One of the province's older communities, Spaniard's Bay, Conception Bay.

Below:
Nature, church and home – the triadic interdependence that down through
the years dictated and shaped the consistency of the province's character.

Clockwise, from left:
Crab pots stacked in the seaport community of Southern Harbour, Placentia Bay; an unforgettable trip to Terra Nova National Park; and, a moment in time – making hay on a late summer's afternoon at Fairbank.

What better way to spend a summer's evening than to be employed in "an affair of luck" on the Gander River.

Previous page:
Who in the seventies would have thought that the day would soon be upon them when the fishery, as a means of employment, would be gone ... for some, perhaps forever? Certainly not these three young men from Jim's Cove.

30

Previous page:

People are the essential elements of any community. They are the agent of production. They, individually and collectively, cause the formulation of social, cultural and physical traits. As well, they are a product of the very community they help build. Much as the landscape of the province has been etched over time, so too have our people – their faces and bodies mirroring character moulded by experience and a life-time of hard work.

Newfoundland – Pre-Confederation

Long before Canada, there was Newfoundland. Europeans knew about Newfoundland long before Giovanni Caboto crossed the Atlantic in 1497, stepped on the first shoreline he found, claimed it for King Henry VII of England, and entered the record books as the explorer John Cabot. There is substantial evidence for Portugal's claims that its ancient mariners plowed the teeming waters of the fish-rich Grand Banks in the 14th and early 15th centuries; the hardy seamen from the Basque provinces of France and Spain chased the great whales off Newfoundland waters.

Norse settlers attempted to found a colony at L'Anse aux Meadows on the tip of the Great Northern Peninsula, but failed, leaving only grass-covered mounds outlining the foundations of their homes and a cloak pin to indicate where the legendary Vinland of the Viking sagas had been.

Europe's first contact with Newfoundland may very well have extended much further back through the centuries: as modern-day mariner Tim Severin proved in 1976, sailing in a leather boat, or *curragh*, from Ireland to Newfoundland, the sixth-century Irish abbot St. Brendan could have travelled across the Atlantic Ocean. In a series of tales later committed to paper, the monk had allegedly spent seven years at sea with a small group of men, encountering a fabulous monster big enough to be mistaken for an island – in all likelihood a whale – and floating mountains apparently made of glass or crystal, a description that suspiciously tallies with how a child might be asked to describe an iceberg.

But no matter what speculation may claim, one fact emerges: that fish first drew first explorers, then master mariners to the future province, and finally settlers to make the New Founde Lande their home. And so began an economic pattern, built largely on the dependence of resources such as cod and other fish species, and much later, wood from Newfoundland's forests, and minerals from the ground, that would continue for centuries.

EMPLOYMENT IN THE FISHERY

It was the fishery that continued to employ much of Newfoundland's outport population during the opening years of the 20th century up to Confederation. However, where there were fishermen, there were also merchants, whose presence in Newfoundland originated in the early days of settlement – indeed, the merchants of Bristol had bankrolled Cabot's voyage. The merchants controlled all imports, and sold supplies on credit to the outport people to carry them through the next season's fishery. In turn, they demanded exclusive rights to the fishermen's catch to be applied against their debt (the infamous "truck system"). The outport men were no longer allowed to sell fish to visiting ships from England or other countries, or to buy goods from them.

It was taken for granted, by both the merchants and the public, that they/the merchants always would be the real rulers of Newfoundland, and this system continued to be part of a way of life for many

Newfoundlanders well into the days leading up to Confederation.

In terms of the overall way of life, the picture described by many older Newfoundlanders, still living, who grew up in the days before Confederation, is a contrasting one. We were poor, but proud, and didn't rely on government handouts the way we do now, and we didn't want to get handouts, says one stream of thought; we had our culture and our identity. Others argue that Newfoundland was destitute, comparable to Third World countries today, and that Confederation was her only saviour.

In a sense, both points of view are true. Many Newfoundlanders were poor; many children went hungry; diseases such as tuberculosis were rampant. However, Newfoundlanders were a proud and culturally rich people, the beneficiaries of a mystique cultivated by writers like Paul West, who called them a "community of Irish mystics cut adrift in the Atlantic." Many of Newfoundland's ancestors were Celts, from Ireland and England's West Country, a dynamic people whose lives spent in isolation and hardship bred an overwhelming sense of place. Even in Newfoundland today can one hear the question of not "where do you come from," but "where do you belong to?"

TUBERCULOSIS

Poverty was a fact of life during the first part of the 20th-century Newfoundland, but also in the rest of North America. The Great Depression had started in 1929, which added to misery, as the market for salt cod had collapsed as soon as World War I had ended.

During the 20s and 30s, one out of three men were unemployed, and many earned an average of $150 a year. Children grew up under-clothed, under-fed and suffered from rickets and beri-beri. Tuberculosis ravaged whole familes and entire settlements. A 1936 government report noted that children sometimes fainted in class from hunger. Since education was not compulsory, many of them never even attended.

In the time of William Coaker, who had rallied the fishermen under the banner of the Fishermen's Protective Union in the early years of the 20th century, fishermen had attempted to fight their social and economic servitude. Now they built their outport houses, picked berries, caught lobster – in those days, only the poorest ate lobster – salmon, and cod, relied on the forests to provide wild meat, and always lived off credit.

LIVED OFF THE LAND

But according to some writers, such as Harold Horwood, many Newfoundlanders were far better off than people living in such places as the *dust bowl* of the West. Outport Newfoundlanders had always lived off the land, and still did so, right through the 1930s. Most of them were very poor; their houses went unpainted; their clothing wore out and was not replaced; thousands of children had no boots or shoes, and some of them stayed out of school because of lack of clothes, but few of them were ever on the edge of starvation. Outports were tightly-knit communities, where residents looked out for each other, shared songs, passed on culture, and treasured their children and elders.

While ordinary Newfoundlanders laboured in the outports, the nation's pre-Confederation politics existed in a complex muddle, with numerous parties and factions coming in and out of power.

SLIDE TOWARDS BANKRUPTCY

Before Joey Smallwood, Sir Richard Squires was the man who dominated much of Newfoundland's political landscape during the years that led up to Confederation. He was a cabinet minister from 1913 to 1918, and Prime Minister from 1919 to 1923, when he resigned amid cries of bribery and corruption, to re-emerge as Prime Minister from 1928 to 1932. Smallwood himself was a devotee of Squires, even through the accusations of corruption.

During Squires' term, Newfoundland began a slide towards bankruptcy, which eventually ended with Britain, with Newfoundland's consent, taking over the nation's government. By 1930, interest charges on Newfoundland's accumulated public debt equalled half the entire annual revenue of the government. Of that $100 million debt, $40 million was accounted for as the unpaid bills of sending Newfoundlanders to fight in France. Faced with complete collapse, Newfoundland turned to Britain to ask for repayment; Britain's response was to suggest that Newfoundland dissolve her legislature to make way for a six-man

commission of British-appointed civil servants. In return, Britain would take over responsibility for the island's debt.

By 1933, unemployment had climbed to 65,000, more than half the entire labour force, and many were forced to rely on government vouchers to buy goods. On Feb. 16, 1934, Newfoundland voluntarily surrendered her independence to Britain for the next 16 years.

However, economic conditions failed to improve, with unemployment rising to 58,000 in 1938 after dropping briefly. The next economic boost would come only with the start of World War II, when both American and Canadian military established strategic bases on the island.

The difference between Newfoundland today and the nation that became a province on March 31, 1949 at 11:59 p.m. seems almost unfathomable, especially to Newfoundlanders born after Confederation. There were few roads; most of them were poorly built and maintained, and people travelling across the province often relied on the ironically-named "Newfie Bullet," a train that took more than a day to get from St. John's to Gander, about halfway across the island. Electric power reached only certain parts of the Avalon Peninsula, the Corner Brook area, Grand Falls, and Gander. Public services such as hospitals, schools, and libraries were few and received little money.

However, Newfoundland would prove that it, indeed, had several assets to offer Canada. Forestry was one of Newfoundland's biggest industries in

1949, with paper mills at Grand Falls and Corner Brook producing much of the world's newsprint; the fishery would also continue to provide much of the world's fish. There was also the potential of millions of dollars of minerals waiting to be mined, and the untapped hydroelectric power of sites such as Churchill Falls.

As well, the Commission of Government set up by Britain in Newfoundland had managed to accumulate a $45 million surplus. Canada's newest province also held the distinction of being the only province with no public debt.

Today, it remains to be seen whether Newfoundland, tagged as a "have-not" province since it became a part of Canada, will lead the country in economic growth in the future, as the province's politicians now forecast. Will the oil-rich Grand Banks create a financial climate akin to Alberta's? Or the nickel-laden deposits in Labrador and Central Newfoundland see a major influx in mining companies?

Economics aside, many Canadians outside Newfoundland recognize that their newest province has made a valuable contribution in terms of culture and heritage to the mosaic that is Canada. Newfoundland is known for its stories, songs, entertainers, artists and authors.

What would Newfoundland be like today if it had not joined Canada? That is a common question, but instead, we should be asking another: what, indeed, would Canada be like if Newfoundland had not joined it?

Sue Hickey

A moment of jubilation:
Joseph R. Smallwood, centre, and Gordon Bradley, left, chatting with federal officials in Ottawa, 1948.

• Photo courtesy of Centre for Newfoundland Studies Archives, Memorial University of Newfoundland

Previous page:

An anchored motorboat – as if keeping watch – on undisturbed water in the community of Gilesport, Twillingate.

Below:

A new age dawns – and all eyes are on Newfoundland as a modern-day colossus nears completion.

Below:

L'Anse aux Meadows – where the history of the New World began.

Adjacent page :
A panoramic view of Curling and area with mountainous backdrop.

Below:
Abitibi-Consolidated mill (and dam), located in the Central Newfoundland town of Grand Falls-Windsor.

Previous page:
Few things equal the quietude of a Newfoundland
lake or pond: Evening on the Terra Nova.

Previous page:
The Town of Grand Falls(-Windsor), founded at the turn of the century by the Harmsworth brothers of England to meet the demand for newsprint in Europe.

46

Confederation

Fifty years have passed since the course of Newfoundland politics was altered forever, and the events surrounding Newfoundland's entry into the Canadian Confederation in 1949 are among the most dramatic in the country's political history.

Newfoundland had been without elected government since 1934 when Prime Minister Frederick Alderdice dissolved Responsible Government under the crushing weight of $100 million in long term debt that Britain refused to re-schedule. The result was a Commission of Government that would rule Newfoundland and Labrador until after the end of the Second World War.

But British authorities had been planning Newfoundland's post-war future well before the end of the war. And their plan was Canada.

In December 1945, British Prime Minister Clement Atlee announced that Newfoundland would hold its first general election since 1932 to elect delegates to a National Convention on its political future.

The National Convention consisted of 45 members elected from 38 districts. The convention began its deliberations Sept. 11, 1946, under the chairmanship of Judge Cyril Fox.

But despite, or because of, the lack of democratic process in Newfoundland since the 1930s, there was a lukewarm response to Britain's decision. Of the 45 delegates elected to the convention, eight faced no opposition in their districts.

The apathy quickly evaporated when the convention began sitting, however, spurred on by radio broadcasts of the convention proceedings. This also played into the strengths of Confederation's frontman, Joseph R. Smallwood, who had been practising public speaking on his radio show, The Barrelman, since 1937.

OFF TO LONDON
AND OTTAWA

At the beginning, convention members assumed that they would discuss "possible future forms of government" only after concluding investigative committee work. However, it took just two months for this plan to change dramatically when Smallwood, a convention delegate from Bonavista Centre, moved that the convention should send a delegation to Ottawa to determine possible terms of union.

In the end, the convention decided to send delegations to London as well as Ottawa, both of them led by the convention's new chairman, who also happened to be a Confederate, F. Gordon Bradley, who represented Bonavista East. (Fox having passed away shortly after the convention was convened.)

Major Peter Cashin, a supporter of Responsible Government, joined the delegation to London in April 1947, which had several meetings with Britain's Dominions Secretary, Viscount Addison. During the meetings, the secretary let the Newfoundland delegation know that if Newfoundland picked Responsible Government, it could count on no economic assistance from Britain. To Cashin, this was evidence of a conspiracy "to sell this country to the Dominion of Canada."

The Ottawa delegation departed in June. In the nation's capital, Bradley and Smallwood schemed to get the Canadian government to draft terms of union which could be discussed by the convention and the electorate. It worked. The pair stayed in Ottawa until October and brought home with them draft terms of union. Back in St. John's, anti-confederates were outraged.

Despite Smallwood's machinations, he soon discovered that he was a minority at the convention. His motion to get the Confederation option on the ballot was defeated. The majority wanted the choice to be between continuing with Commission of Government for another five years or a return to pre-1934 Responsible Government. Smallwood dubbed the anti-Confederates "the 29 dictators."

But it appears Smallwood had an ace up his sleeve – the support of Mother Britain, which stepped in and politely informed the convention that Confederation would be on the ballot after all.

Voters in Newfoundland were to be given three choices: return to Commission of Government, Responsible Government, or Confederation with Canada.

With little enthusiasm for a return to direct rule by Britain, the battle lines were drawn between Canada and Responsible Government.

The advocates for Responsible Government were further splintered between the Responsible Government League, led by Cashin, and the Economic Union Party, led by St. John's businessman Ches Crosbie. Onside with the Crosbie group was Don Jamieson, who later went on to become a cabinet member in the federal government of Pierre Trudeau.

With the stakes raised, so too was the fever pitch of the debates at the National Convention.

At one point, Cashin, who represented St. John's West, accused Confederates of being traitors to their country, leading to this testy exchange with Smallwood:

> **Smallwood:** *Mr. Chairman, isn't that hitting a bit below the belt? If I were to tell Major Cashin that he was a traitor to his country, he would not like it.*
>
> **Cashin:** *No, I would drive you through the window.*
>
> **Smallwood:** *Yes, well now you are 50 pounds heavier than I am, and if I weighed as much as you do, and if it was the other way around, maybe I would throw you out of the window. I think that's hitting below the belt.*

Cashin: Well, that's my opinion, and I'm entitled to express it.

This little tiff was but a prelude to the bitter debate that followed.

The St. John's paper, The Herald, backed Crosbie's plan for economic union with the United States. An editorial two months before the first ballot stated: "The destiny and welfare, not only of the present, but of generations unborn, are the responsibility of every man and woman voter in Newfoundland."

The pro-Confederates also churned out the heavy propaganda. A leaflet distributed under the headline, Mothers, Read This, claimed: "Once we get Confederation, we know that never again will there be a hungry child in Newfoundland. There will be hungry children under Commission of Government. There will be hungry children under Responsible Government."

ANTI-CONFEDERATE

The Roman Catholic Archbishop, E.P. Roche, strongly supported an anti-confederate line, reflected in the archdiocese's newspaper, The Monitor.

Despite the heavy rhetorical barrage, the first ballot on June 3, 1948, did not produce a majority result. Responsible Government ended the first vote with 44 per cent, Confederation 41 per cent and Commission of Government dropped after garnering a mere 14 per cent.

The stage was set once again for a final ballot July 22, 1948, between Confederation and Responsible Government. This time, Confederation received 52 per cent of the vote, the remainder opting for Responsible. Canada would soon welcome its 10th province.

The voting patterns revealed just how divisive the contest was. During the first vote, two-thirds of voters on the Avalon Peninsula voted for Responsible Government. On the second ballot, every district but one off the Avalon voted to join Canada.

While a majority of the province's Catholics did live on the Avalon, a case can be made that geography and economics influenced the voting patterns more so than religion.

After the vote, all that was left was to negotiate the Terms of Union with Canada. Then as the clock ticked down to midnight on April 1, 1949, Newfoundland turned to face west.

Smallwood insisted that Newfoundland join Canada on March 31, not April Fool's Day. The federal government wanted the deal to come together with its fiscal year-end.

Newfoundland's first Lieutenant Governor, Sir Albert Walsh, swore in Smallwood as the first premier. The first election as a Canadian province was held May 27, 1949.

David Sorensen

Pages 50-53:

A smooth frozen Fosters Pond, Barr'd Islands, more often than not, caused people to come together on a frigid winter's afternoon for hours of enjoyable skating ... when otherwise they might have stayed indoors; coastal communities such as Gaultois, Hermitage Bay have long extracted the resources of the sea to maintain their local economies; and, wide-angle view of Frenchman's Cove – jutting determinately into Bay of Islands.

Clockwise, from left:

Reflected image of the Come By Chance oil refinery; though perched along rugged coastline, communities have their own distinctive characteristics, even though common central element is often a place for worship; and, caulking the boat before setting out to sea in the spring of the year was a tedious but necessary chore.

Abitibi-Consolidated, Grand Falls Division uses the Port of Botwood, Bay of Exploits to ship newsprint to U.S. and European markets.

Pages 56-58:
A full moon helps light the ski-runs at White Hills, Clarenville; the motorboats tied up to the wharf of an abandoned fishing community appear incongruously opulent; and, below, once a major contributor to the economy of the province, the Town of Buchans is determined to again make its mark.

Previous page:
  The airport Town of Gander has always played a pivotal role
  in helping break the province's isolation and allowing
  expansion into the global community/market.

60

Previous page:
Schooner traverses the waters of Notre Dame
Bay, 1919. Ominous clouds develop in the
distance.

62

Clockwise, from right:

Joseph R. Smallwood holding Volume II of the Book of Newfoundland which he compiled, edited and published in 1937; Gordon Bradley and former premier; and, spring of 1948 - Joey with bundles of telegrams and petitions from people all over Newfoundland urging the British government to put Confederation with Canada on the referendum ballot.

• Photo courtesy of Centre for Newfoundland Studies Archives,
Memorial University of Newfoundland

Page 64:
Joseph R. Smallwood campaigns to have Newfoundland join Confederation.

• Photo courtesy of Centre for Newfoundland Studies Archives,
Memorial University of Newfoundland

Clockwise, from left:

Joseph R. Smallwood with his beloved Encyclopedia of Newfoundland; Prime Minister Lester Pearson visits the former Town of Windsor; Joey addresses Kiwanis Club, Grand Falls-Windsor; and, comparing election notes – portentous at the very least.

Photographs – R-B files

Clockwise, from bottom:
Premier Clyde Wells calls on former premier; a proud moment for Joey when Russian president Alexei Kosygin vists; the 1959 IWA strike tests the former premier's mettle; and, JRS presents chain of office to one of a long line of mayors of the former central town of Windsor – the first town to be incorporated in the province.

Photographs – R·B files

A man of irony

Joseph Roberts Smallwood may appear as a fictional character in Newfoundland writer Wayne Johnston's *The Colony of Unrequited Dreams* – nominated for numerous major literary prizes shortly after it was published – but the reality of his life is the stuff of which classical drama is made.

The former premier, who died in 1991, lived a life constructed of contradictions. He would often enter two opposing philosophies and build another from the hybrid of the two, which in turn would meet yet another, and so the process goes.

Some men are "men of iron" – Smallwood was a man of irony.

"He was a man who, in his time, played many parts: a union organizer who eventually became a strike breaker, a journalist who carried on a running battle with the press, an agnostic with a passion for collecting materials on the life and teachings of the English evangelist John Wesley," stated Harold Horwood in *Joey: The Life and Political Times of Joey Smallwood*.

"Smallwood was also a self-proclaimed socialist whose private friends included the right-wing premier of Quebec, Maurice Duplessis, the Portugese dictator Antonio Salazar, and the most controversial president of the United States, Richard Nixon."

It's only fitting, then, that Joey Smallwood would become both the most loved, feared and hated of Newfoundlanders during his career as a politician who changed his country's history and held power continuously, almost unchallenged, for 22 years and eight months.

GAMBO CLAIMS JOEY AS NATIVE SON

Smallwood's hold on Newfoundlanders is still mesmerizing. Even the community of Gambo, where he only spent a few brief months for the first part of his life, continues to claim him proudly as a native son - proud enough to raise nearly $100,000 to commission sculptor Luben Boykov to mould his likeness in metal, preaching to the stones.

One who had plenty of time to become more than familiar with Smallwood's strengths and weaknesses because he had worked with the man for much of his political career is Ed Roberts, a former justice minister in Premier Clyde Wells' government.

Roberts got his start as an executive assistant to Smallwood, later served in his cabinet as public welfare minister, and eventually won the leadership of the Liberal Party after the premier resigned following his loss to Frank Moores' Conservatives in 1972.

Roberts observed that Smallwood was possessed of great strengths, but as in the case of many men and women saddled with the sobriquet of "Great," his weaknesses were significant as well - perhaps the reason which accounts for the paradoxes that defined Smallwood in life, both in his activities and in the stroke that robbed him of the power of speech in 1984.

"I first got to know him relatively well when I was working for six summers as a summer reporter with CJON Television," recalled Roberts. "He was available, accessible, we all had his home number, he was glad to hear from anyone. I later became involved with campus organizations, where I came to know him quite well...He was a very complex man, with very deeply held beliefs, and prodigious talents. He was compassionate about Newfoundland and devoted to making things better.

"He had faults, but there was also his unswerving commitment to the province."

BORN ON CHRISTMAS EVE, 1900

If Smallwood had created the new province of Newfoundland by Confederation in 1949, Newfoundland in turn could claim responsibility for creating his persona. As Richard Gwyn astutely pointed out in *The Unlikely Revolutionary*, Smallwood's childhood was unhappy enough to give him a head start towards becoming an exceptional man.

"He came from that traditional source of revolutionaries, the lower middle class, and he was lucky enough to be born in Newfoundland, and not in a more ordered and affluent society which had no need of a saviour."

While Smallwood often claimed affinity with outport Newfoundlanders by citing the community of his birth, Gambo, he actually only spent the first six months of his life there. He was born on Christmas Eve, 1900, to Charles and Mary Ellen Smallwood, when the elder Smallwood was working as a woods surveyor at Mint Brook, just outside Gambo.

Soon after Smallwood's birth, the family moved back to St. John's. His childhood could be best characterized as "wretchedly poor," a life marked by frequent moves from one shabby house to the next, as Charles Smallwood shuttled from job to job, and meals frequently consisting of nothing more than bread, potatoes and tea. With his background and education, stated Gwyn, Charles should have done better - he was educated at Methodist College and came from a family with a prosperous boot and shoe factory - but he destroyed himself with drink. This gave rise to scenes where Mary Ellen Smallwood often struggled to sober up her drunken husband, hence Joey's stance for much of his life as a rabid teetotaler.

However, Joey would soon be given an opportunity to rise out of that background of poverty, when his Uncle Fred, manager of the family boot and shoe factory, paid for the boy to go to Bishop Feild College. This was where the St. John's merchants sent their sons if they couldn't afford to send them to public schools in England.

At Bishop Feild he established a lending library of

juvenile books, and also led a successful "strike" to protest the food served in the College dining room. He would later become a socialist after a chance meeting with George Grimes, a member of Sir William Coaker's Fishermen's Protective Union.

He was noted as a bright student, but didn't always do well academically: he often daydreamed, filling scribblers with the names and titles of Newfoundland Prime Ministers. Then, according to Gwyn, he would write his own name with a flourish: "The Rt. Hon. Sir Joseph Smallwood, K.C.G.N., P.C., M.H.A.

"I regret, of course, not having had more education, but it might have made me more a trained seal, less sure of myself. Action might have been lost in the pale cast of thought," said Smallwood.

Another point of irony, perhaps, in that long list of paradoxes that characterized Smallwood. This was the small man who questioned the role of higher education in his own life, yet established Memorial University and for a time, provided free tuition for the province's sons and daughters. In 1915, the future premier, having run afoul of the rules of College, left to work as a printer's devil with the city newspaper the *Plaindealer* and six months later, as a hand typesetter with the *Spectator*. He later joined the *Daily News*, working as a circulation clerk for the next two years. During this time, he wrote anonymous letters and articles under the pen name "Avalond" for the *Fisherman's Advocate*, a daily put out by the FPU.

"I romanticized reporting as if it were the best job in the world," he said. "When I became a reporter, I was absolutely on top of the word. I just lived and breathed and ate my job."

In October 1918 he answered a "Reporter Wanted" ad in the St. John's *Evening Telegram*; he got the job and would stay there for two years before he resigned to work for the *Halifax Herald*.

Smallwood eventually made his way to New York where he wrote for the socialist newspaper *Call*, and became active in the Socialist Party. He was persuaded to return to Newfoundland by a labour leader and friend, John P. Burke, to reorganize Local 63 of the International Brotherhood of Pulp, Sulphite and Paper Mill Workers at Grand Falls, and built the membership from about 100 to 900 in a few months.

Smallwood then decided to form the first Newfoundland Federation of Labour, an organization for all Newfoundland unions. He later organized Local 64 of the above-mentioned union in Corner Brook, and also 600 railway workers who had been threatened with a wage cut.

He married Clara Oates in 1925, and in mid-1926 – "unemployed, restless and wishing to experience the intellectual life of English socialism," stated the *Encyclopedia of Newfoundland and Labrador* – he left for England, where he immersed himself in Labour politics and went to numerous political and philosophical meetings.

He returned to Newfoundland in 1927, moving to Corner Brook, where he was Sir Richard Squires' district campaign manager. To break into politics, he decided to start the *Humber Herald* in Corner Brook, which had been newly established as an electoral district; however, he did not run as Squires had decided to run there himself.

The paper later collapsed under a mountain of debt in 1930, but before then, Smallwood was well-prepared for political life. When an election was announced in 1928, he ran in Bonavista South, where he lost 812 votes to 3528.

By 1936, Smallwood had moved his family back to St. John's, where he returned to writing, publishing *The Book of Newfoundland* in 1937. He also had a show on VONF, "The Barrelman," based on a column he wrote for the *Daily News*, where he talked about local history and folklore, and later operated a piggery outside St. John's in 1939. In 1943, he set up another piggery in Gander.

POLITICAL OPTIONS

While visiting Montreal in 1945, Smallwood read about Britain's proposed plans for Newfoundland's constitutional future. Prime Minister Clement Atlee had announced that Newfoundlanders would elect 45 people to a national convention to investigate its financial and economic condition, and to recommend to Britain what forms of government Newfoundland should adopt.

Smallwood considered the political options – which included Confederation with Canada – and decided he would stand as a candidate to the Convention, to which he was elected.

The Convention first met on Sept. 11, 1946, where Smallwood became – in the public eye – leader of the Confederate cause.

In 1947, the Convention received the Terms of Union from Canada; in 1948, a first referendum vote was inconclusive. After a second referendum, Confederation took 52.3 per cent of the vote. In the course of 22 years as premier, Smallwood won six general elections. The seventh, in 1971, resulted in a tie.

The first few years saw Newfoundland's integration with Canada; after that period, Smallwood worked on economic development within the new province, concentrating on industrialization, educational and public works reforms.

The one-time socialist was now looking for outside interests to invest in Newfoundland, forging deals with controversial American business people such as John Sheehan and John C. Doyle, who each built projects with substantial government assistance. Smallwood was also lobbying Ottawa for public works funding, which he got, bankrolling the paving of the Trans-Canada Highway across the Island and the development of hydro power at Bay D'Espoir.

He also achieved the goal of developing the hydro power at Churchill Falls, realized when the British-Newfoundland Corporation signed a long-term deal with Hydro-Quebec – a deal which would later haunt Smallwood while he was alive, as well as tarnish his memory. Many Newfoundlanders felt that the premier had "sold out" to Quebec, with the latter reaping the benefit of the monies from the development.

In 1966, Smallwood's Liberals once again claimed victory in the provincial election, taking all but three of the 42 seats. Elected at this time were several young politicians who would later become familiar faces to Newfoundlanders decades later – Ed Roberts, John Crosbie, Bill Rowe and future Premier Clyde Wells.

He resigned the leadership in 1972 after the Conservatives narrowly won the provincial election, and Roberts was elected the new leader of the Liberal Party.

Smallwood briefly returned to politics in 1975, with the Liberal Reform Party, and was elected as the MHA for Twillingate, but resigned his seat in 1977 and retired from politics.

He continued to write, publishing two more volumes of *The Book of Newfoundland*, as well as *No Apology from Me* and *Dr. William Carson, The Great Reformer*. He also embarked on a vision long dormant in his mind: *The Encyclopedia of Newfoundland and Labrador*.

Sadly, however, after the publication of volume two of the *Encyclopedia*, the man whose oratorial skills were the hallmark of his personality was struck by a cruel irony: a stroke in September of 1984, one that deprived him of his speech and his ability to write.

Still the Smallwood Heritage Foundation, organized by a group of people to raise funds for the *Encyclopedia*, managed to bring Smallwood's vision to completion, eventually publishing its entire six volumes.

But Smallwood did not live to see the whole of the *Encyclopedia* make it to print. On Dec. 18, 1991, Joseph R. Smallwood died, shortly after volume three was published, and a state funeral was held Dec. 21.

Smallwood's contribution to Newfoundland history may be even more momentous than one can imagine. What if there hadn't been a Joseph R. Smallwood? Would Newfoundland still be its own nation, a British colony, or a possession of the United States?

It's likely that Confederation may not have been possible without Smallwood, but the latter's existence as the pivotal politican of Newfoundland's history may not have come around without the former.

"Who knows? Events make the man, or does man make the event?" asked Ed Roberts. "Confederation in 1949 was a fortuitous combination of a man and a time."

Sue Hickey

71

Pages 72 and 73:
At certain times of year, the bushplane was, and still is today, the only means of getting to the more remote parts of the province, like Postville, Labrador; and, a day's work begins at Herring Neck.

Below:
The richness of the Newfoundland character and its people has evolved over time and from the simplicity of remote setting. A resident of Nain, Labrador planes away the unneeded to expose essential form.

Pages 75-76:

An iceberg, resembling retracted image of the province, floats in the waters of the North Atlantic; and, houses in the White Bay community of Hampden flood to water's edge taking on elongated reflections.

Clockwise, from left:

Few places in North America come close to equalling the beauty of the pristine landscape of Labrador. The Pinware winds its way to the Atlantic; and, bottom photo, keeping your own garden was a way of life for most Newfoundlanders; however, today, it is more the rarity.

Previous page:
   Homes nestled in the hills of Exploits.

80

Previous page:

Remember When – This award-winning photograph of Elsie Barbour by Falk has the signature of an earlier day.

With a slim majority voting to join Canada, it was quite understandable that there were mixed feelings April 1, 1949 when the new province woke and realized that "we" were Canadian citizens. Some were jubilant, while others flew flags at half mast, and wore black arm bands.

Within weeks Newfoundlanders had elected their first provincial government, which, after a hard-fought campaign, resulted in a Liberal government with party leader Joseph R. Smallwood becoming premier. We also elected our first members of parliament.

In time change took place: The Newfoundland Ranger Force, which up to that time had been policing outside the capital (where it was done by the Newfoundland Constabulary), was taken over by the Royal Canadian Mounted Police. The majority of Rangers were offered positions with the Mounties.

Customs' duties on goods imported from Canada were no longer payable. This was a bonus as many in the province did their shopping by way of the catalogues.

It was no longer necessary to have a medical clearance (and a chest x-ray in hand) when moving to "Canada."

At the same time a number of regulations already in place in Canada were now also enforced here.

Perhaps the biggest change – used as bait in garnering the Confederation votes – was the promise of increases in welfare payments, children's allowances, widows' and old-age pensions, veterans' pensions, and Unemployment Insurance.

Every aspect of Canadian government services became available, and many of our services were integrated into Canadian operations – such as the Canadian Broadcasting Corporation, postal and telegraph services, Canadian National Railways, coastal boat services, etc. The Canadian Armed Forces, which had had a major presence here during the war, set up stations, with bases and airports under their command.

While some matters relative to goverance of the province came under the jurisdiction of the province itself, others, of which the fishery was perhaps the most important, became the responsibility of the federal government. National organizations began to spread to this province, allowing us to contribute to and learn from their experiences.

The provincial government saw fit to adopt a new flag, and chose the Union Jack – forsaking the Newfoundland flag (the Red Ensign with the Newfoundland insignia).

EQUALIZATION PAYMENTS

One of the first major changes brought about because we were now a province of Canada, was the way the union affected the province's financial status. Income taxes and other taxes were paid to the federal government, and in return we received grants (sharing the Canadian wealth) in the form of equalization payments. This new source of income was a lot more than we might ever have been able to raise on our own. It provided our government with the opportunity to build roads, hospitals, schools, and many other facilities, which in turn raised our level of education, health, employment, and social services, and helped end much of the isolation which had existed.

Unemployment Insurance was introduced as a cushion for those out of work; but, all too soon, it became abused and developed into a way of life for many. Within a few years, Medicare was introduced, starting with coverage for the children, and later extended to all.

INCREASED ACTIVITY

The quality of life had improved for all, the health of the population was much better, and new jobs were developed because of the increased activity across the province. Exploration in Labrador resulted in the start of the great iron ore mining at Labrador City and Wabush; and, the Churchill River was harnessed, providing power to the province of Quebec and the United States, as well as meeting local needs. The Trans-Canada Highway was built (and thereafter the trans-island railway was discontinued). Resettlement was encouraged and the residents of

many smaller outports moved to larger communities where there were better facilities, and perhaps even more opportunities.

As Canadians, many thousands of Newfoundlanders joined the Armed Forces, the RCMP, and other government agencies; and, with enthusiasm and the benefit of a better education, they also found jobs in many other parts of the world.

WAR AND ITS EFFECT

A study of world history will show that many of the great and significant advances in technology are brought about during the course of wars. This is particularly evident of World War II; and, where this one great event is concerned, we benefitted here in Newfoundland as much as anywhere else.

Gander and Goose Bay airports became stepping-off points for Atlantic crossings by planes during the war – and this extended into civil aviation after the war. Gander, especially, was an international airport and saw a flow of planes landing and taking off daily. It was a new industry. At the same time, this province was by then linked to all of North America by air service. We no longer felt the isolation of the past.

Labrador began to open up, and construction of the Trans-Labrador Highway was undertaken, allowing access to the rest of Canada via Quebec. When completed, it will extend to the Strait of Belle Isle; and, possibly, there will be a fixed link in the future, to connect with the island of Newfoundland. Further discoveries, such as Voisey's Bay, hold great promise, as does the construction of the Lower Churchill power project, which will provide even more electrical power. It must not be overlooked that there are other great rivers in Labrador which may one day be harnessed, if only for the pure water which presently drains into the Labrador Sea. This may prove to be essential to North America, which is fast running out of fresh water.

DOWNSIDE

However, while one tends to count the benefits, there is another side to be considered. The federal government has been responsible for the fishery in Canada, and a few years ago had to declare a moratorium to halt the obliteration of the cod fishery. Thousands of people were suddenly thrown out of work.

For years the fisherpeople had been warning department officials that over-fishing was taking place and had to be stopped. As Canadians, we had seen our territorial limits extended from three miles to 12 miles, and then later to 200 miles. But it was not enough. Foreign ships were fishing in our waters, and with their new technology, they were destroying everything from the sea-bed up. In a few short years the damage was done.

The federal government produced funding to assist those who were put out of work by the moratorium, to maintain them during a period of retraining. Problem was, we did not have 'other' jobs. In desperation, more than anything else, we found that there were other species of fish which could be caught and sold, and slowly a new fishery began to develop, one that must be nurtured and cared for.

Beyond the fishery, modern technology was also taking its toll in the woods, where power saws and harvesters are now displacing manual labourers. And, similar stories can be told where other industries are concerned.

EDUCATION

Meanwhile, we had made a great effort in the field of education. Memorial University had grown into a major institution, and a second campus, Sir Wilfred Grenfell College, was established at Corner Brook. A medical school was built in St. John's, and a nursing school was established in Corner Brook. The health care system was enlarged and improved, and tele-medicine was introduced in the province. A number of private post-secondary colleges sprang up providing further education in new fields. Nor have we been left behind in the electronic age, for many of our young people are now in the forefront of the new technologies.

The traditional seal fishery has been hurt badly by the anti-sealing campaigns. It is sad that the federal government, once again, has not recognized how important it has been to our people over the years. The seal herd is now some six million strong, and, so we are told, requires a regular culling to prevent further downsizing of the cod fishery.

UNEMPLOYMENT HIGH

As we approach the end of the 20th century, we find that while we have made tremendous progress in some fields, we have also lost ground in others. Our unemployment rate is the highest in Canada, and we benefit from the employment insurance and social services, which we could never have been able to sustain on our own. We also find that we represent a mere one and a half per cent of the population of Canada, and while we have a voice in the affairs of the country, we also know that it is a mere whisper. We know that we have benefitted from a health care system which we could not have subsidized on our own – but we also are having trouble funding the ever-increasing costs of the system.

SMALLER POPULATION

We are aware of the falling birthrate and the out-migration from our province, which is having a grave effect on our transfer payments. In turn, the resultant changing demographics have affected our education system, and we are seeing school closures and teacher lay-offs. Our population has dropped in the past few years from a high of almost 600,000 to 543,000 in

mid-1998, and the outflow continues as our people leave to find employment where they can.

After 50 years of Confederation, half the population of Newfoundland and Labrador has never known that they might have been anything but Canadian citizens. They were born and grew up as – and are proud to be – Canadians. The older folk have many memories of the independence we gave up in 1949 and the way of life as it was lived in the 'old days.' No doubt, they will often debate the pros and cons.

To properly and completely look at '50 years of Confederation' would require a mass of research and result in a major tome. For this dissertation, one can only highlight a few of the things which have affected us as a province and as individuals.

In the final analysis, we each have to answer such questions as: Has the quality of life improved? Has our life expectancy increased? Have we developed a pride in being Canadians? Could we have accomplished what we have today if we had continued on our own?

While we are often too quick to criticize and downplay the positive, in the end there can be little doubt that Confederation has been good for us. We could never have accomplished what we have today – at least not on our own.

Dr. Noel Murphy

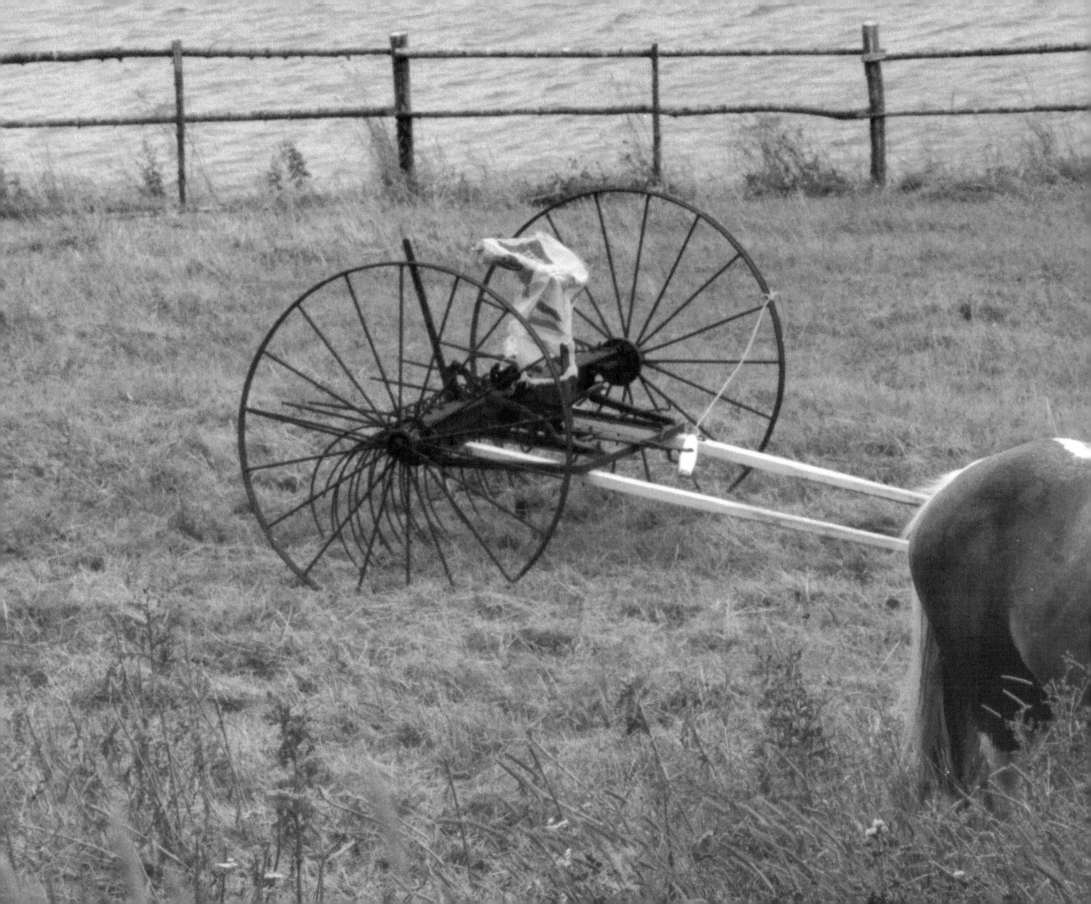

Pages 87-89:
Port Hope Simpson and mountainous backdrop; and, enjoying
a summer's day in Cape St. George, Port au Port Peninsula.
Below:
From-the-reeds view of Western Brook Pond.

Previous page:
> The settling beauty and calm of Glovertown.

Below:
> An earlier day – with Jim Strong of Little Bay Islands.

Right:
> Conception Bay community of Brigus.

Previous page:
Town of Springdale which serves as a service
centre for many communities along the shores
of Green Bay.

94

The people known throughout the world as Newfoundlanders have the historical mark in this country as a people of such uniqueness that, for them, the concept of distinctness defies definition. The Confederation of the Dominions of Newfoundland and Canada fifty years ago was a marriage of two independent states. Newfoundland, by democratic process, surrendered its status as nation with all that such a transformation implies to the status of province within the nation Canada. The marriage contract itself and the process which delivered it will be forever debated within the province as long as there are two people on the island left to engage each other. This is how it is in Newfoundland. This is how we remind each other of five hundred years of social evolution in a land that gave nothing in an easy manner but was so terribly difficult to give up.

Newfoundland
paid its dues...

Newfoundland did not come into Canada a pauper and destitute, nor should it do anything but hold its head high. Newfoundland paid its dues on the battlefields of two world wars as an independent nation and distinguished itself in the blood of boy-fishermen on the fields of Europe.

Newfoundland brought into Canada enormous natural resources and a labour force that continues to this day to create and contribute in every town and city across this great land. It gave to Canada control of an ocean so vast and so infinitely rich that it soon became one of this nation's greatest economic bargaining chips on the international stage.

Newfoundland gave and it received as well from a country whose generosity cannot be parallelled throughout history. Canada received its newest province with dignity and equality.

The sea and the
land defines us...

It is an incredible stroke of good fortune to have come from a people "in whose bodies old sea-seeking rivers roar with blood" (W. Johnson: The Colony of Unrequited Dreams) and marry into a family of regions and peoples as diverse and distinct as make up this country. The sea and the land defines us as Canadians. To stand on the most easterly point of North America and look West over the single most fortunate land mass on the planet that makes up Canada is nothing short of wonderful: as in the Newfoundland expression, "She's a wonderful grand country."

For those of us fifty years of age and older to be able to say proudly "I was born a Newfoundlander" is indeed special. To now add that "I am a Canadian" is to lay claim to a status that is respected and envied throughout the peoples of the world.

To have grown up in a Newfoundland outport like Brigus is to have exquisite memories of small boats and the fishermen who went out in them each morning to the staccato sounds of the make-and-breaks fingerprinting each one's identity. To smell the ocean and the twine, to hear words spoken as in rhyme, the sounds of boats readied in the Spring is to conjure images to be treasured as rare coins. These are reflections of the past, of a life that was as harsh as it was romantic.

We, as Newfoundlanders, whether from the island or the Labrador part of the province, must never forget where we came from. We must, however, seize the future with all the vigour and tenacity that is our birthright. Our future is Canada's future. We are Canadians. We have a right to be here. We are proud to be here. We chose Canada.

Judge Robert A. Fowler

Pages 99, 100:

The Town of Gambo, where Joseph R. Smallwood spent a few brief months for the first part of his life; and, a summer's day at Greenspond, Bonavista Bay.

Left:

The distant hills and houses of Harbour Le Cou emerge from a veil of fog.

Below:

Notre Dame Bay community of Brown's Arm.

ACKNOWLEDGEMENTS

To the writers – Sue Hickey, David Sorensen, Dr. Noel Murphy, and Judge Robert Fowler – who took the time to research and write the articles for this book.

To Charlie Falk, whose more obvious contributions to the exercise, made the hours of 'selection' an enjoyable experience.

To those many employees of Robinson-Blackmore Printing and Publishing on whom I had to call for their advice and expertise; especially, to Calvin Jeans, Terry Fisher, and Melvin Burry; and to my wife, Delores Ennis, whose careful eyes helped ensure that the product was top quality.

To the president of Robinson-Blackmore Printing and Publishing, Derek Hiscock, who gave unwavering support for the book.

Ron Ennis

Adjacent page:
FINAL REFLECTION – Things that will endure forever in our province are the irresistible forces that have the power to exalt and unify. Over the years they have inspired the noblest deeds of valour and sacrifice. Photo, inspirational images in the Town of Hillgrade.

Below:
The town of Musgrave Harbour, as seen from the beach.

ROBINSON **BLACKMORE**
Printing and Publishing